A Sense of Place: Fiction in the Agrarian Tradition

Joe C. Ross

TROY STATE UNIVERSITY PRESS
TROY, ALABAMA

This publication was made possible by a National Endowment for the Humanities grant to the Alabama Public Library Service for its *Perspectives: The Alabama Heritage* project.

A Sense of Place: Fiction in the Agrarian Tradition by Joe C. Ross

COVER ILUSTRATION By George Burton Dodge

Library of Congress Number: 78-56163
ISBN Number: 0-916624-18-8

Dedication: To Thomas Daniel Young,
Southern gentleman and scholar

Joe Carl Ross was born in Amory, Mississippi, and received his B.S. at Tennessee Polytechnic Institute, his M.A. at George Peabody College, and his Ph.D. in English at Vanderbilt University. His dissertation is entitled "Robert Penn Warren and the Negro." Having presented a number of papers on them and other Southern writers, he is also especially interested in William Faulkner and Flannery O'Conner. Dr. Ross has been a member of the English Department at UAB since 1967. He has served as chairman of the English Department and, since 1975, as assistant dean of the School of Humanities. Dr. Ross's wife, Upha, is the manager of Blackburn's in Brookwood. They have three children, Larie, 25, Mike, 21, and Andria, 20. In addition to his love for reading, gardening, and photography, Dr. Ross enjoys playing tennis, basketball, and bridge. The Rosses are active in the Christian Church (Disciples of Christ). They enjoy membership in a square dance club.

A SENSE OF PLACE: FICTION IN THE AGRARIAN TRADITION

Joe C. Ross
University of Alabama in Birmingham

When we think of the South as a section of the country, the image that immediately comes to mind is one of an agrarian region. When we think of the Southern past, the image is one of plantations with white-columned houses and white-blanketed fields. When we think of the people other than the slaves singing as they labor or the leisured planter class sipping mint juleps, we envision hunters roaming the virgin woods. Such images of life in the South are oversimplified, but they indicate the extent to which agrarianism dominates our concept of the South. The agrarian life was and continues to be a significant aspect of the Southern way of life.

Beginning with Thomas Jefferson and John Taylor, Southern writers have declaimed the virtues of the agrarian existence. Man on the land is an ideal to strive for, a goal to extol. Living close to nature means being close to God and in contact with universal truths and eternal values. The Southern belief is that man is most aware of what manhood entails and most aware of the deeper meaning of life when he has established a close relationship with the land. If the Southerner does not establish this relationship through planting and harvesting, he does so through camping, fishing, hunting, or other outdoor activities.

In 1930 twelve Southerners – among them two Alabamians, Herbert C. Nixon and Frank Lawrence Owsley – published a collection of essays called *I'll Take My Stand.* An agrarian manifesto, this work opposed industrial capitalism and warned against the increasing mechanization of modern life. The manifesto especially lamented the fragmentation and destruction of individuality accompanying an industrial dispensation and extolled strong response to a changing way of life. Such a response is readily understandable because of the dominant agrarian pattern, which of itself fostered individualism, a pattern reflected in the qualities of self-reliance, strength and pride traditionally attributed to the Southerner. The twelve Southerners known as the Agrarians foresaw a difficult life for the Southerner in an increasingly complex society in which individuality would more and more be sacrificed to conformity amid the increasing pressures of urbanization and industrialization.

Alas, the fears of the Agrarians were well founded. No one needs to be reminded concerning the trends toward more complexity in society, more control by government and less possibility of individuality. We still associate the best values of life with closeness to nature, for who of us does not dream of owning a cabin on the lake or spending a vacation or at least a weekend in the seclusion of a state or national park? Yet the number of those who have close contact with nature decreases yearly. The farm population continues to decline in the United States. From 1970 to 1976 it dropped 15%, by 1.5 million, at which time only 8 million people (1 out of 26 Americans) lived on farms. As is true of all sections of the United States, trends toward urbanization and industrialization in the South continue.

Elements of the agrarian tradition reflected in the imaginative literature of Alabama writers include the importance of the land and of the family, a sense of place, and the close relationship between living on the land and being close to God. Agrarian writers, the authors of Alabama being no exception, reflect the tradition of agrarianism by presenting in their fiction themes on one or more of the following topics: (1) a sense of place, (2) the importance of family, (3) moral and religious values, and (4) man on the land. Writers occasionally do not agree with the traditional values associated with agrarianism. For example, rather than showing man on the land as a beneficent arrangement, an author may portray the hardships of the situation. Or man may feel estranged from God rather than close to him, and the family may break apart because of the difficult life on the farm. More often than not, however, the family gains coherence and strength from facing and overcoming the problems on the farm. Forces alien to agrarianism may be responsible for the most severe problems of the man on the land. The depression, for example, created untold suffering, a situation not attributable to the man-land relationship. On the whole, Southern writers portray the values they find inherent in an agrarian way of life.

The following discussion emphasizes the way in which certain Alabama fiction writers have treated the themes which recur in the agrarian tradition. In order to be of greater value to the reader, the commentary is based on fiction which is currently in print or easily available in Alabama public libraries.

The reader of the fiction discussed below will discover that a sense of place is important in the following: Stewart, *Through the First Gate;* Brown, *Stars in My Crown;* Sanguinetti, *McBee's Station;* Warren, *Whetstone Walls;* Murray, *Train Whistle Guitar;* Kelley, *Alabama Empire.* The image of place is not necessarily that of a farm or farm life. The place in *Whetstone Walls,* for example, is a community – not a town, but a country settlement. In *Alabama Empire* it is an Indian village, while in *Stars in My Crown,* the place is a small town. In all of those novels, however, place is important to the characters. It is a significant force in shaping their values and their lives. The quality of their lives is enriched by the contact which they have with their place. A sense of place gives them a feeling of belonging, a sense of identity. They have roots.

The family is a particularly important influence in the following: Stewart, *Through the First Gate;* Brown, *Stars in My Crown;* Sanguinetti, *McBee's Station;* Warren, *Whetstone Walls;* Murray, *Train Whistle Guitar;* Coleman, *Orphan Jim;* Borden Deal, *The Other Room.* The family provides stability and order; it inculcates moral values and advocates proper modes of thought and action. The strongest emphasis on family is in *Stars in My Crown,* in which the grandfather teaches sound thinking and right acting to his grandson and to the community not only from the pulpit but also by example. When the family begins to break apart, as in *McBee's Station,* moral chaos results and the strength to face the problems of life is diminished. In *Orphan Jim,* the traditional family is replaced by an unorthodox interracial family arrangement, including a one-time prostitute who now serves as a mistress for a man with a traditional family in another town.

Moral and religious values are important elements in at least four of the novels discussed: Stewart, *Through the First Gate;* Brown, *Stars in My Crown;* Warren, *Whetstone Walls;* Borden Deal, *The Other Room.* However, only in *Stars in My Crown* does organized religion find a sympathetic author. The other novels present the characters as being turned off by the church. The agrarian life, including family and natural influences, provides the characters with a high standard of moral and ethical values, but their contact with organized religion results in rejection of the traditional approach.

The agrarian ideal of man on the land is treated in several novels discussed below: Stewart, *Through the First Gate* (anti-farm); Sanguinetti, *McBee's Station;* Warren, *Whetstone Walls;* Coleman, *Orphan Jim* (anti-farm); Borden Deal, *The Other Room.* The contact of the characters with nature may be nothing more than the tending of potted plants or greenhouse flowers, as in *Whetstone Walls* and *McBee's Station,* but that contact is beneficent, providing delight or solace. The novel which most strongly shows man on the land in the traditional sense is *The Other Room.* Through the family of tenant farmers portrayed in the novel, Borden Deal shows how the family's love for the land and closeness to the soil bring beauty and purpose to their otherwise drab and work-filled lives. Their ambition to own the soil burns within them like a glowing coal, and when that ambition at last seems capable of fulfillment, they are happy and content as they were never before.

In the novels selected for consideration, however, closeness to the land does not always have a beneficent influence on the farmers. In *Orphan Jim* the land is too barren and the struggle too severe for the two orphan children. They must escape to the city. One may argue that they do not give the country a fair trial, but the fact remains that they do flee the country and go to Montgomery, where with diligence and luck they make a success for themselves. Had they stayed on the farm, it is not unlikely that the grinding poverty that they faced would have destroyed them, as it did their parents.

As noted later, *Through the First Gate* is, like *Orphan Jim,* an anti-agrarian novel, for the dreams and ambitions of Tom MacAllen lie in distant countries and cities, not on the farm that his mother dislikes and that his father stubbornly wrestles with. And the people who are native to the area are poor whites, proud, prejudiced and individualistic to the point of self-destruction. The novelist may recognize that dehumanizing poverty exists in the country as well as in the meanest of city slums.*

*For a discussion of the agrarian and his character traits, the reader will find the thirty-page Chapter 2 of W. J. Cash's *The Mind of the South* (1941) interesting and informative.

INDIVIDUAL WORKS

Borden Deal, *The Other Room* (1974)

The depression meant for the Sword family hardships and backbreaking work, but their love for the land and their deep family attachments bring them through. But not without losses. A member of the family dies, and this death is enough to shake Christian Sword's faith in God. Christian, the narrator, is 15 years old and as a result of a series of brush arbor gospel meetings feels that he has received the Call to preach. Although his father had at one time also considered preaching as a profession, neither he nor his family have even been churchgoers. They are decent, respectable, God-fearing people, however, and their real faith is in the land. As tenants their great dream in life is to be able to own land. Having lost his farm as a result of the depression, the father, Lee, says with yearning and determination, "One of these days, I'll own my own land again." One of the two times that Christian remembers seeing his father truly angry was the day when the sheriff brought a piece of paper taking away his land. (The other time occurred when he came upon a man beating a mule with a trace chain.)

When it seems that owning land again is a strong possibility, Lee and his wife Jimmie watch the dawn break as they look out on what they hope may soon be their own land. This is the hour of their life Christian "most likes to remember."

Yet love for the land, strong as it is, does not mean that land ownership is to be gained at all costs. Pride and independence do not permit one to accept a marriage arrangement without love. Conscience is not to be sacrificed to comfort. In the end, Chris, molded by the land, leaves it for the other room. Old now, he returns to tell us the story.

It is a touching and beautiful story. Not only do religion, the family, and the land play a part, but there is also the story of Chris's lust. Initiated into sex by an older woman, he comes to love one his own age and is caught in a triangle. He cannot give up one, and he won't give up the other. Refreshingly direct and candid in his narrative style, Christian tells the reader, "You won't read here any attempt to excuse myself."

Deal is an excellent storyteller. The dialogue, for the most part, sounds authentic, and the suspense of the plot line keeps one reading. Chris decides that there is both good and evil in life as he has known it. Chris at times feels that life is life-in-death, but the reader comes away aware that the good is more abundant than the evil.

Joe David Brown, *Stars in My Crown* (1947)

Stars in My Crown is a novel of family and of place. The action occurs in a small town called Walesbury in Jones Valley during the years before World War I. It is a first person account by John, the grandson of the parson Josiah Doziah Gray. Though the story takes place during the formative years of the boy, it is the grandfather who is the real focus of the story. John is the observer, reporting the statements and actions of the grandfather. John's parents died when he was young, and he was fortunate to live with his grandparents, for his grandfather is a wise and godly man. He understands human nature, and he trusts completely in God to assist in straightening out the affairs of man.

The close relationship between the grandmother, the grandfather, and John makes the novel one of family. And the close relationship of all citizens of the town makes it a novel of place. The townspeople share their stories about past events in the town, and they are concerned about what happens to each other. For example, when a couple after ten years of marriage finally are to have a baby, all of the townspeople eagerly look forward to the event. When the father drowns in a flood as he goes for the doctor and the baby is stillborn, the mother in her shock refuses to accept the baby's death. For the rest of her life, she takes an imaginary baby strolling in a buggy which had been presented to the couple as a gift by the men where the husband worked. The children in the town call her "Crazy Ella," but the townspeople are sympathetic with her and indulge her eccentricity. When another baby in the town is made an orphan, the Ladies Aid considers giving the child to Ella to take the place of her imaginary child.

However, the grandfather persuades the group that the fantasy child is more of a comfort to Ella than a real child would be, for the fantasy child has been idealized by Ella, and the perfect child, Grandpa thinks, could not be replaced by a real baby. The Ladies Aid is persuaded to give the baby to another couple in the community who ask for it.

In addition to the grandparents and their grandson as an example of the closely knit family in *Stars in My Crown,* there are the parents of Chloroform Wiggins, who have lived for twenty years in a house built on a raft, complete with pigs and chickens and a garden plot. On their raft they float down the river, and then when the notion to go upstream strikes, they persuade some ship's captain to let them hitch to his boat. Their isolation on the raft would suggest the ultimate in family togetherness.

Chloroform got his name because his mother liked the sound of it. She enjoyed the sedative effect of chloroform when she was giving birth to her son, and when she was told the name of the sleep-inducing substance, she decided to name him for it. Like Crazy Ella, Chloroform is an eccentric – at least from the point of view of the townspeople. After the sudden death of his parents when he is sixteen, he leaves the life on the river. Of the twenty acres of land which he buys he uses only one-half acre, on which he has a house just like the one on the raft, with a garden plot in one corner and a pig pen and a chicken coop in the other corners.

Chloroform is content with life on the small plot of ground. When he goes in to the store to purchase a fishhook, the men gathered in the store tell him he is letting the community down because he is content and wants nothing and lets the rest of the people do his worrying for him. Teasing him, they try to persuade him to pick out some item to purchase from the store so that they can buy it for him, and then he can begin worrying about paying the money back. When he can find nothing in the store he wants except a fishhook, they ask him to look through the catalog. But again he wants nothing other than the fishhook.

There are enough people like Jim and Ella in the community to suggest that like Winesburg, Ohio, Walesburg, Alabama, is a community of grotesques. But the narrator's perspective is governed by the advice on writing that his grandfather gives him.

That advice is not to write an ugly book. The grandfather admits that it is true that each person has some bad within him, but he thinks that the good outweighs the bad and that one should emphasize the good. John says he must tell things as they are, but he promises to look for the good. Joe David Brown's novel is a fulfillment of this promise.

Babs Deal, *The Reason for Roses* (1974)

The Reason for Roses is a nostalgic story of family and place in a small town in North Alabama in the 1930s. Spencer's cousins, Weightsill, Brook, Marles, and Raleigh, spend the summer with her, and it is the last summer of their adolescence. To them, it is a wonderful summer, but also a terrible one, for as typical adolescents they are at one point happy and lively and at another, depressed and self-conscious. An indication that they are growing up and leaving their childhood activities is the difficulty which they have deciding on a summer project. They eventually decide to have a scavenger hunt and hope that the youth who always seems infallible will not win the hunt. However, no matter how they rig the hunt, they are unsuccessful: as usual, he proves his superiority.

Spencer relates the story in the 1970s, forty years after it happens, and from her viewpoint at that later time, she also comments on changes in the town and the fate of the cousins. The ice plant which they visited in the 1930s no longer exists, for the refrigerator makes the demand for ice non-existent. A laundromat now pollutes the stream which in the 1930s bubbled with water which you could drink. Spencer and one or the other of her cousins talk in the 1970s about how it was in the 1930s.

They have many meals, which Spencer delights in telling about. The meals are served by a black maid and are cooked by a genial and matronly black cook. The members of the family talk unceasingly, sitting on the screened-in porch, reminiscing about the past. It is a matriarchal family, presided over by Dandy, the grandmother, with assistance from Aunt Vic and Aunt Fletcher and Aunt Zora, who is named for an Indian princess, the last of her tribe.

And there is the odor of roses, for Dandy has many flowers and talks to them years before it became a fad to have so many house plants and carry on monologues with them. The reason for roses is to remember and to yearn for the distant past, for it was a time of growing up, and we forget the pain, the family quarrels and unpleasantness and remember how it never was. It is lovely now, and it is pleasant to cling sentimentally "to family, places, root, security."

John Craig Stewart, *Through The First Gate* (1950)

Through the First Gate takes thirteen-year-old Tom MacAllen through the difficult years of growing up. Enabling him to pass through the first gate are a strong family life and the values Tom learns from the family, the guidance he receives from Charlie, an old black man who works for his father, and the virtues he gains from close association with nature through life on the farm and through hunting. The final stage of his growth to maturity comes in spite of his weaknesses, including a lack of confidence. He is accepted by a group of boys, friends of his cousin, with whom he spends some time in town during the summer.

Rufus is Tom's arch enemy, and while the two boys share an agrarian background, the contact that Tom has with the urban environment that summer seems to tip the scales in his balance. Although Tom's strengths and virtues are molded by his family life and by his contact with nature, he is unable to cope with Rufus and the conflicts that Rufus poses for Tom until he has spent the summer vacation in the small town where his relatives reside. There his weaknesses are tolerantly accepted, and he finally surmounts his sense of being an outsider. Through the interlude in the town, Tom is provided the key to win over Rufus and therefore to pass through the first gate.

The sense of moral order for Tom does not come through organized religion. His awakening sexuality creates within Tom a sense of guilt, but after agonizing over this and attempting to talk with his father and with Charlie about it, he finally makes his own peace with God. He decides that he doesn't care what the preacher says, and he ends up indifferent to organized religion.

Mainly because his family is looked upon as outsiders in the small farming community in which they have inherited some property, Tom, taking his values from his family, is an outsider with his peers. The rednecks, as his father calls them, are prejudiced and suspicious. Tom's father fights the KKK when the group comes after Charlie. Had Tom been willing to join with the junior Klansmen on the occasion when, led by Rufus, they play hookey from school, he would have thereby gained acceptance. He does play hookey, but he refuses to join as a Klan brother.

The basic approach of the novel is anti-agrarian because of the way that the poor whites are portrayed. Their contact with nature is not beneficial, for they evince a stubborn pride, a dislike and distrust of outsiders, and an unyielding prejudice toward blacks. The pride that Rufus exhibits brings about tragedy, and the pride his father shows compounds that tragedy.

However, Tom's life is better because of his contact with nature. His life on the farm includes labor, but it also provides opportunities for hunting, at first under the guidance of Charlie, through which activity he gains a "serene sense of timelessness and certainty." But the struggle with his fellow students and the mutual lack of understanding create within him a desire to escape his environment. Though he is offered the leadership of the group of boys at school at the beginning of the upcoming school year, he is not interested. He is glad that he has only one school year remaining; after this, as his father has promised, he will be permitted to go to school outside the community. He thinks of all roads leading *away*. Maturity for Tom, having passed through the first gate, involves moving on. Significantly, his dreams are not dreams of an agrarian life. Perhaps the first gate is not simply the passage from childhood to maturity but the passage from an agrarian existence into another country. This life on the farm has prepared him to meet the future.

Albert Murray, *Train Whistle Guitar* (1974)

Train Whistle Guitar (1974) by Albert Murray is a beautifully written book narrated by Scooter, a black man who returns in memory to his youth spent in a small town near Mobile. The reminiscences evoked about the past include school days, misty rainy winter days with grown-ups telling about the great "Juvember" storm and other stories as they sit around the fireplace. Story tellers include Unka JoJo, Sawmill Turner, and Uncle Walt.

Scooter and Little Buddy Marshall lead an adventurous life. They hop a train in order to ride along with Luzana Cholly, a legendary figure, a traveler and singer, and an ex-prisoner. The two youths discover a body in the swamp and then watch as it is disposed of by three men. The men, the boys surmise, are moonshiners and the body that of a revenue agent. The boys see the results of a tragic love triangle, when Bea Ella Thornhill slashes Beau Beau Weaver because he is making time with Miss Clementee Mayberry. Bea Ella, after serving time in prison, is known as Red Ella because she acts like a middle-age church widow. From a vantage point in a tree, the boys witness the break-up of a Saturday night party at which Stagolee Dupas is playing. Deputy Sheriff Earl Joe Timberlake thereafter breaks up no more parties, for when he starts to kick the keys off the honky-tonk piano, as he had done so many times before, Stagolee says, "Hold it right there." The deputy is found shot the next morning, and rumor places the blame on bootlegging activities.

Adventure in *Train Whistle Guitar* is less important than the colloquial, realistic way in which the story is related by Scooter. The reader tends to respond, "Yea, man, that's the way it was. I've been there." The dialogue sounds like real people talking, and the reminiscences are those of a real person, an optimistic and alert youth who years later recalls how it was. Family is important to him. The family is especially proud of Scooter and his accomplishments in education, and the memories that he retains of the family life and family relationships are warm and sustaining.

Not to be forgotten also is Scooter's sexual initiation, which he narrates in a delightful manner.

Scooter is fascinated with the tales told by the people in his community, and the reader is in a similar way fascinated with Scooter's account of these stories and of his own experiences in his salad days in South Alabama.

Lonnie Coleman, *Orphan Jim* (1975)

Orphan Jim begins with Trudy Maynard, age thirteen, and her brother Jim, age seven, forsaking the farm for life in the city, where with luck and responsible application of their talents, they make their own way in life. Trudy's father began as a clerk in a dry goods store. After his wife inherited family money, they bought a farm. The attempt at farming failed, for Sheldon Maynard did not give farming a serious trial. He did not know how to farm, nor was he interested in learning. An author following the agrarian tradition would have shown Maynard's contact with nature on the farm to be a healing and beneficent contact. It was not, for he soon lost the farm and rented a piece of "sorry land," continuing to go downhill from there, ending up a drunkard and deserter of his two children after his wife's death.

Perhaps a novel in the true agrarian tradition would have shown Trudy making a valiant plea with her landlord to remain as a tenant on the farm, putting all her efforts into building it up into a productive piece of land, eventually purchasing it for Jim and herself, sending Jim away to school to become a doctor or a lawyer. Eventually, in old age she would sit on her porch looking out over her fertile acres, her grandchildren playing happily nearby. But the agrarian tradition can't always win.

The plight of Trudy and Jim after their father's desertion is truly piteous. Having once been told by Uncle Earl that he would help them should they need to call on him, Trudy runs away to Montgomery, where she lives with Aunt Olive and their son and daughter. Aunt Olive has to be one of the most selfish and hard-hearted creatures in literature, concerned as she is with her own two precious children and worried about the money it takes to feed extra mouths. After two or three days, Aunt Olive persuades Uncle Earl to make arrangements for the two waifs to go to an orphan's home. Instead, they again run away. Luckily, they finally come across some kindhearted people. This happenstance, together with hard work, is all they need to survive the depression. The lucky breaks keep coming their way. Trudy, having passed her 34th birthday, tells us the story.

Although the story shows the break-up of the family based on kinship, it shows another family replacing the traditional one – one based on love and concern for one another. When the family founded on love, which rises above racial barriers, is destroyed by the death of one member, a transformed Trudy and Jim survive and prosper. The basis for the ability to survive seems to come from the love that was experienced in the racially integrated family. In the beginning of the novel, Trudy, ill-tempered and argumentative, is mean to Jim, calling him "Orphan Jim" for spite. As she shoulders responsibility, she becomes more mature in speech and action. Always a girl of pluck, Trudy is a willing and able worker; her capabilities and efforts see her, and Orphan Jim, through. Life may offer little to amuse or entertain, except an occasional motion picture, but it has appropriate and just rewards for those who persevere.

Elise Sanguinetti, *McBee's Station* (1971)

Mrs. McBee's son, a taciturn and gloomy John Bedford McBee, Jr., is in his thirties. He lives with his mother, spending his time writing, sending off manuscripts, and receiving rejection slips. Mrs. McBee thinks it is time he got a real job, and when he gets a job as an English instructor at a nearby college, she is pleased that he is following in his father's footsteps as an English teacher but displeased that it is only a part-time job.

Mrs. McBee regrets the changes that have occurred in the small town of Ashton, Georgia, and the surrounding country where she lives. Much of the land had belonged to her father and his father before him. Now sixty-four, she operates a greenhouse and works hard to make ends meet, has done so since John Bedford McBee, Sr., died suddenly twenty years ago. But the land has been sold and broken into housing developments, inhabited by, in Mrs. McBee's judgment, trashy and uncouth people. As horrible as thoughts about her own death are visions that her property will be taken over by her next-door neighbors, the Flemmings. Mr. Flemmings works at a government job, and Mrs. McBee regrets that her tax money is being spent to support trashy people like him. Mrs. Flemmings has worked for Mrs. McBee in her greenhouse for eleven years, and though Mrs. McBee finds her outspoken fundamentalist religious ideas repulsive and her loud and incessant talking irritating, especially her delight in dwelling on unfortunate and tragic happenings, she has come to find comfort in her companionship.

Mrs. McBee's great satisfaction comes from working with her plants. She thinks of them as her children, the kind she had never had, cheerful, playful, endearing. The plants are "God's glory surely," she thinks. Her concern for the land and her love for her plants are, of course, vestiges of the agrarian tradition in the 1960s.

Mrs. McBee's self-righteousness also brings her to condemn "new money," those who "butcher the king's English," and those who come into "her church" (Episcopal) and sit in "her pew," flaunting their Catholic ways or possessing still their Baptist beliefs. Her condemnation of these interlopers also extends to their hypocritical actions, for she wonders how they can worship, considering their unethical business practices and immoral conduct.

Mrs. McBee takes pride in the fact that her family and her husband's family come from prestigious forebears, from land-owning and socially prominent people. Her family is "all from Virginia," and her husband's family was a "South Carolina family." Very much concerned about family background, she almost bursts with pride when at long last John Bedford invites a girl friend for dinner. Because the girl's name is Johnston rather than the more common Johnson, Mrs. McBee is sure that the girl is a member of a long-established and well-to-do family of the community. She makes elaborate plans for an impressive dinner, even asking her cleaning woman, Willie Washington, to serve at dinner. When Helen Johnston appears, Mrs. McBee is devastated to discover that she is black.

Mrs. McBee's sense of the importance of family is exemplified at another point in the story when she calls her daughter, Mary Hughes, and her husband to come to visit when she can no longer cope with John Bedford. Yet she does not want a confrontation and suggests to John Bedford that they have come just to have a "nice family time" and that in time of trouble they need to "stick together." John Bedford takes the opposite point of view, for he wants nothing to do with Mary Hughes or her husband. The family is breaking apart, and it requires more than a quaint sixty-four-year-old woman who lives in the past to keep it together.

Mary Hughes does offer her a garage apartment and says that if it does not hold her furniture, she and her husband will be happy to keep the antiques in their house for her. But Mrs. McBee realizes the insincerity of this proposal.

In addition to Mrs. McBee and her family, her neighbors, the Flemmings, are another representative family at McBee's Station. Mrs. Flemmings is very proud of her son-in-law, Buster, Jr., who, though he was forced to marry Lojean because she was pregnant, has redeemed himself by proving to be such a hard worker. He has even taken night classes at the college, and Mrs. Flemmings knows he will really make something of himself. Mr. Flemmings takes him into partnership, establishing a filling station and a garden supply store and, finally, a greenhouse in competition with Mrs. McBee's. It is a family enterprise that brings the threat of ruin to Mrs. McBee.

The other daughter in the Flemmings family, Bertha Mae, also poses a threat for Mrs. McBee, as the latter sees John Bedford, Jr., and Bertha Mae together and fears that John Bedford will take up with her, perhaps even marry her, and that the McBee property will be engulfed by the Flemmings family. When the Flemmings accuse John Bedford of impregnating Bertha Mae, Mrs. McBee's worst fears seem on the verge of fulfillment.

The best part of the novel has not yet been mentioned. That is the delightful realism of the dialogue. Sanguinetti knows Southern speech, and with a minimum of misspelling, she presents the dialect with accuracy and humor. Mrs. McBee may disapprove of those who "butcher the king's English," but Mrs. Sanguinetti adds much to the telling of a story by showing just how they do butcher it.

Welbourn Kelley, *Alabama Empire* (1957)

Behind the scenes in *Alabama Empire,* a long but fascinating historical novel set in New York City, Alabama, and Philadelphia from 1789 to 1793, is the struggle between the Georgia settlers and the Creek Indians for the Alabama territory. The leader of the Creek nation, Col. McGillivray, comes to have high regard for Dr. John Fyfe, narrator of the novel, who is sent by President Washington to be doctor to Col. McGillivray. The move benefits the United States, as Dr. Fyfe's influence persuades Col. McGillivray to sign a treaty with the United States, thus giving up his alliance with Britain and effectively neutralizing Spain as a force in the territory.

The political developments are sufficiently detailed to allow the reader to appreciate the growth of the territory toward statehood. However, the human relationships as portrayed in the novel, including a romantic triangle, will be of greater interest to the general reader than will the political matters. Especially interesting also is the portrayal of family concerns among the Indians. Marriages of young females often occur as young as nine or ten, so parents usually have a voice in these affairs. Yet even with arranged marriages, adultery is seldom practiced and is severely punished. Col. McGillivray has more than one wife, as is the custom of the Indians, but there is no conflict between the two wives, as they live in different parts of the territory, one at the seat of government and trade at Little Tallassee and the other near Mobile. Not only is there no conflict, but there is no animosity or envy between the two, though one of the wives is better loved and in fact exercises subtle control over Col. McGillivray, even to the point of having picked out the second wife.

The Georgians are interested in settling the Alabama territory for farming and hunting purposes. The land is valuable, and as the new nation grows, the settlers continue to move into the territory illegally. Thus in this novel can be found struggle for the possession of land, which could be said to be the beginning of the agrarian tradition.

What is given here about the novel does not do it justice, and is even misleading, as the larger part of the action occurs outside Alabama, and many interests of the characters lie in matters that have little to do with the Alabama territory; on the other hand, the motivating force for much of the action is in the control of the

Alabama trade, which also involves leadership of the Creek nation. At the end of the novel Dr. Fyfe and his bride, who are honeymooning in Scotland, dream of the beautiful hills and streams of Alabama, reciting in a lilting song the Indian place names of the territory.

Lella Warren, *Whetstone Walls* (1952)

Lella Warren, in *Whetstone Walls* (1952), emphasizes the family and family relationships. Focus is eventually placed on certain characters in the novel, but as the novel begins, the reader cannot be sure who the chief characters are, since the family rather than individuals is emphasized. The immediate Whetstone family is large, and there are many relatives. The author revels in relating the preparations for festivities and family get-togethers, along with the events themselves. The family members are sociable, and there are few conflicts.

It turns out that Rob, the third of four boys in the Whetstone family, which also includes an adopted girl, is the leading character. In 1883, when the novel begins, Rob is twelve. Throughout the novel, he feels rivalry with his older brother, Upshur. Upshur's air of confidence and his ability to persuade others to let him have his way are traits that Rob envies. The names of the two boys are fitting: Upshur is sure and usually comes out ahead in any difficulty, sometimes taking what Rob wants. But does Rob really want one thing or another, or does he merely think he wants it because Upshur strives for it and obtains it? The rivalry involves competition for small possessions – and in one instance for a scholarship – when the two are boys. It involves the opportunity to pursue a career and the winning of a girl friend and wife when they become young men. Only on the last page of the novel does the reader discover the outcome of this last rivalry. The rivalry of the two boys never becomes an open conflict; it is merely one element in the novel, adding interest and suspense. Family is the most important element. There are aunts and uncles and cousins, and they visit and celebrate and take excursions. When Rob goes away to college in New Orleans, he is met at the station by a distant cousin. He spends time with the cousin's family. He also immediately pays a visit to an aging Cousin Armand. The reader receives the impression that Rob has not really moved away from the little Alabama town in which he lived, for he is still among relatives.

The title of the novel refers to the importance placed on family relationships, for the members of the family are like stones and hold together like walls, the family relationships being the cement of those walls. Ms. Warren obviously delights in telling of the family activities. She is at her best in recounting the hustle of the preparations for parties, the comments of one person to another, and the plans that they tell each other for their lives in the future.

While family relationships are emphasized in *Whetstone Walls,* the novel also gives the reader an impression of what life in a small Alabama town is like. It is a comfortable life. The families all have servants. The minister and his family are referred to as poor; yet they also have servants. Their poverty is reflected mainly in their being unable to afford a piano, although their daughter has her heart set on a musical career. This is not to say that the Whetstones do not work, as they keep themselves occupied around the house in some way or other. Rob's sister, for example, grows flowers, and Rob also seems to have a green thumb.

Rob's love for growing things is one of the few indications of the importance of agrarianism in this novel. He loves the soil. Returning from New Orleans for a visit, he reaches down and digs up two handfuls of soil, burying his face against it. "Good old red clay," he says.

On the other hand, those who are bound to the soil may not feel as Rob does; Ms. Warren refers to the "back-breaking labors" of the young boys who come to school from the farms. Listlessness and hunger characterize them, and at noon or recess they often do not have the energy to play, but return to their desks, put their heads down and sleep until school takes up again. The lunches which they bring to school are cold and unappetizing.

However, this scene is only a brief one in a novel filled with happy family activities. *Whetstone Walls,* one is almost surprised to realize upon reflection, is another story of a youth coming into maturity. There are some problems in this passage from one age to another, but the problems are minimal because of the strength of family ties.

Truman Capote,* *A Tree of Night and Other Stories (1956)*

One of the stories in Truman Capote's *A Tree of Night and Other Stories,* "Children on Their Birthdays," concerns a child whose father is in prison and whose mother is a lost and helpless person. The child speaks and acts in a very mature manner, paying no attention to the childish antics of the boys who wish to impress her. They stand in awe of her when she insists that they treat Rosalba, a young black girl, like a lady, and they gladly assist her in her entrepreneurial efforts.

The child's name is Miss Bobbit; she is ten years old when she is run over by the six o'clock bus. And the small Alabama town in which she and her mother had come to live about two years ago will never be the same. Miss Bobbit was very unusual, very intelligent, and a very good organizer and leader, but the attraction which she held for the young boys in the town, especially the good friends Preacher Star and Billy Bob, was a troublesome one. For she will not state a preference for one or the other, and she will not take them seriously. Wise and mature beyond her chronological age, Miss Bobbit commands the respect and (even) admiration of the whole town. Her one mistake seems to be failing to hear the bus when it rounded the corner as she ran with outstretched arms toward Preacher Star and Billy Bob to give them a goodbye hug.

Another story of a small Alabama town is "Jug of Silver." The narrator's Uncle Ed Marshall has a drugstore that loses business when a competitor sets up across the street. Then he thinks of giving chances on guessing the amount of money in a wine bottle filled with coins. The possibility of winning the money creates quite a stir in the community. A family moves to a farm three miles from town, and a boy in the family hears of the excitement and comes to make a guess. He can make only one

*Although Truman Capote was born in New Orleans, he spent a number of years with relatives in Alabama, and the stories discussed here are set in Alabama.

guess, because you get to guess only with a twenty-five-cent purchase, and he has only a quarter. After months of studying the bottle, the boy, Appleseed, makes his guess.

The story not only reflects life in a small town, but it is also a story with emphasis on family. Appleseed is not interested in getting the money for himself but for his little sister Middy, who has a dream of being a movie star. But she cannot be one as long as her teeth are crooked. The solidarity of the family is shown further when Appleseed's brother gives him the quarter needed to guess the amount of money. His brother makes the money by playing the fiddle at a wedding.

In addition to the two stories discussed, two other stories in the collection, "My Side of the Matter" and the title story, take place in the South, and other stories have Southern characters. They could easily be Alabama settings and characters. In addition to the fact that Capote's characters are Southern, most of them are eccentric or unusual. Capote is a deservedly popular author, and his style of writing is a rewarding extra for the reader. Though not discussed here, *The Grass Harp,* a short novel by Capote, made into a Broadway play, has agrarian subject matter.

ADDITIONAL WORKS BRIEFLY NOTED

The novels discussed above are by no means all the works of fiction on the general subject of agrarianism written by Alabama authors. The following list provides additional examples. Further readings in the novels listed will reward the reader with the knowledge that Alabama writers have done and continue to do good work.

Bell, Robert E. *The Butterfly Tree* (1959) [Emphasis on place]

> Peter Abbott is a young man growing up in Moss Bayou, Alabama. Living with his great-aunt, he is drawn into a strange search for the Butterfly Tree, the end of the search being the finding of fulfillment and the end of innocence.

Brown, Joe David. *Addie Pray* (1971) [Emphasis on family]

> In spite of the fact that the country was in a depression in the 1930s, being a con artist at that time was a lucrative business, we learn from the adventures of Addie and Long Boy.
>
> Addie's mother dies in an auto accident, and Long Boy persuades the relatives to let him take Addie to an aunt's to live. But Addie, an eleven-year-old with charm and a quick intellect, suspects that Long Boy is her father and works on his sympathy, preferring to stay with him and pursue a series of adventures as con artists. They try going straight once, when they sell pictures of F. D. Roosevelt in Birmingham after the President's visit to the city, but it is too tiring, so they continue through Alabama, Tennessee, Mississippi, Arkansas, and Louisiana in a series of adventurous swindle games. The movie *Paper Moon* is based on this delightful story.

____________ . *The Freeholder* (1949) [Emphasis on family]

Born in an English prison, Horatio Tench comes to the United States in 1816 and rises from plantation overseer to owner. He sends four sons to fight in the Civil War.

Campbell, William Edward March [William March]. *A William March Omnibus* (1956) [Emphasis on place]

Contains his first novel and some fables and short stories. The novel is *Company K* and deals with World War I. Most of the stories are set in the South.

____________ . *Come in At the Door* (1934) [Family, Place emphases]

A small boy grows up in the South amidst the grotesque, the eccentric, and the horrible, but the matter-of-fact style tempers the strangeness, transmuting ugliness into beauty. The boy witnesses the hanging of his black friend, whom he has betrayed, and lives under the shadow of this gallows.

____________. *The Tallons* (1936) [Family, Place emphases]

Two brothers in a small Alabama town fall in love with the same girl, with tragic consequences.

____________. *The Looking-glass* (1943) [Emphasis on place]

Reedyville, Alabama, mostly before 1917, with an array of abnormal characters psychoanalyzed.

____________. *The Bad Seed* (1954) [Family, Place emphases]

A suspenseful horror story of hereditary evil as it appears in Rhoda Penmark, a murderess at age eight. Her spendid manners impress the adults in the town (Reedyville?), but other children are afraid of her.

Coleman, William Laurence [Lonnie Coleman]. *Adam's Way* (1953) [Emphasis on place]

Gives the attitudes and prejudices of the small town mind. The town is located in Alabama, and the characters include an old Southern scholar, a retired school teacher, and a young black girl.

__________. *Beulah Land* (1973) [Emphasis on family]

The Kendricks own Beulah Land, a Georgia plantation, but their overseer, a free black, part Indian, ambitious and unscrupulous, vows to acquire adjoining property and leaves the Kendricks to devote his time to this new estate. The time of the novel is 1800 to 1861.

__________. *Clara* (1952) [Emphasis on family]

Lillian is a selfish and determined Southern woman who drives her husband to drink and into the arms of their black servant, Clara.

__________. *Escape the Thunder* (1944) [Emphasis on place]

Coleman's first novel, the setting is in Montgomery, Alabama, and the story is about life among the blacks in that place. There is violence, cruelty, and passion. Written without emphasis on race problems and without condescension.

__________. *King* (1967) [Emphasis on place]

A boy, his dog, and the boy's aunt and uncle and their friends in a small Georgia town (500 population) during the 1920s. The boy and his dog are inseparable. An orphan being raised by his aunt and uncle, the boy has everything Mark Twain would expect a country boy to have.

Covin, Kelly. *Hear That Train Blow* (1970) [Emphasis on place]

A documentary novel based on the 1931 Scottsboro case which was recently in the news because of the court case against a TV network brought by one of the two white women involved. The novel has to do with civil rights, court cases, the South, race relations, and the role of the Communist Party in the United States.

Deal, Babs H. *Acres of Afternoon* (1959) [Emphasis on place]

Her first novel. About the conventions of small town life, the differences between surface appearances and reality in an Alabama town. A "woman's novel" in that it describes problems many women seem especially to delight in reading about: romance of young people of the upper middle class.

__________. *High Lonesome World: The Death and Life of a Country Music Singer* (1969) [Family, Place emphases]

The country music singer and songwriter Hank Williams is the prototype of the hero of this novel, narrated through the use of interior monologues by his mother, his manager, his two wives, and other people in his home town. A series of flashbacks reveal that the hero died of "too much living, too much sorrow, too much love, too much alcohol and drugs."

__________. *The Walls Came Tumbling Down* (1968) [Emphasis on place]

A skeleton of a baby is found in an air shaft of a sorority house that is being razed in a small Southern university town. It is determined that the baby must have been placed there twenty years earlier, in 1944, when the air shaft was open for repairs. During that time nine coeds, seven of whom are now respectable matrons in the community, lived in the house. Each of the seven panics, suspecting the others of guilt.

_____________. *Night Story* (1962) [Emphasis on place]

Explores the lives of several people during one night (with flashbacks) in the town of Bellefonte.

_____________. *The Grail* (1963) [Emphasis on place]

A football coach at a Southern university dreams of a ten-game sweep. Complications come when his knight – oops! – football player falls in love with the coach's wife.

_____________. *It's Always Three O'Clock* (1961) [Emphasis on place]

Eileen Holder, a youth in a small Alabama town, Bellefonte, in the 1920s, sees many changes in American life from her high school days to her life as a grandmother at Cape Canaveral, Florida. The mood of a Southern town's culture and its local eccentricities are portrayed, along with the townspeople's reluctant acceptance of progress.

Deal, Borden. *The Spangled Road* (1962) [Emphasis on place]

Domino, the clown, ready to retire at age fifty-two, instead becomes half owner of a circus, plagued with equipment failures, accidents, deaths of animals, and the rains and winds.

_____________. *The Advocate* (1968) [Family, Place emphases]

John Bookman, a lawyer in a small Southern town, takes as a client the town's richest citizen and a power in the state, who believes she will soon die and wants him to defend her will. The provisions of the will will either strengthen or destroy the lives of her four children, who have all lived in their mother's shadow all their lives. Bookman also must deal with the problem of an illegitimate son, a problem raised by

Bookman's political enemies to thwart his political ambitions.

__________. *Interstate* (1970) [Emphasis on place]

Who cares if the interstate highway obliterates Blackwater swamp, the last refuge of the ivory billed woodpecker? Roxy Deberow, blond, sexy, and unfulfilled, does. And she persuades the project engineer, Drew Kyler, rugged, handsome, and also unfulfilled, to help her fight the nasty bureaucrats.

__________. *The Insolent Breed* (1959) [Place, Family, Religion emphases]

The life and times of a Tennessee Valley community. Tells of a family over three generations and their battle with the evangelists of the town. Recreating time and place and people in a strong way, it is the story of music and sin in conflict with guilt-ridden pilgrims who walk a straight and narrow path.

__________. *The Least One* (1967) [Emphasis on family]

Poverty, struggle and triumph in Bugscuffle Bottoms in 1932. Because of low cotton prices, Lee Sword loses his land, and the family must resort to tenant farming. The twelve-year-old son narrates the story, an almost nostalgic one of the Depression.

__________. *The Winner* (1973) [Emphasis on place]

John Bookman (*The Advocate*) makes it to the governor's mansion, where he is possessed by a vision which he calls The Great Venture, in keeping with which he invites all citizens living out of the state to return home. "We need you." He means blacks, too, and he attracts the interest of a black secret society that is antagonistic to white men making conciliatory gifts to blacks.

__________. *Dunbar's Cove* (1957) [Emphasis on family]

The Dunbars, a Tennessee farm family, put up a fight against the TVA to save their home. The characters are people of dignity and simple worth, not depraved poor whites or degenerates.

__________. *The Tobacco Men* (1965) [Emphasis on place]

The growth of the North Carolina tobacco industry involves a power struggle (with masked raiders) for *the* tobacco man Owen Knox. Based on a scenario by Dreiser for a movie script of the tobacco story. Takes place in North Carolina and Kentucky after the Civil War.

__________. *The Loser* (1964) [Emphasis on place]

A struggling young lawyer with a country background agrees to run for governor – and agrees to lose. The five most powerful men in the state want him to draw votes away from the three-time governor so that their own candidate can win. He finds in the race a great many sexual requirements and also is bitten by the bug to run in earnest. With more women and more money, he might do it.

__________. *Dragon's Wine* (1960)

Squire Duncan rules over a settlement known as Duncan's Bottom, a near-feudal barony of lumber and cotton. Homer Greaves, the orphan whom the Squire takes in, has a strong ambition to own all of Duncan's Bottom.

__________. *Walk Through the Valley* (1956)

Deal's first novel. A hillside farmer, Fate Laird, finally achieves his ambition to own a valley farm, but in his conflict with evil, he finds the price is too high to pay. He retains his integrity, though the walk through the valley is a hard one.

Henderson, George Wylie. *Ollie Miss* (Reprinted 1973) (1935)

Ollie Miss is a young black and a mystery, appearing suddenly on Uncle Alex's cotton plantation and asking for a job. A strong character, Ollie arouses the animosity of some of the women and the admiration of the men. At length she finds peace and purpose in life.

Huie, William Bradford. *In the Hours of Night* (1975) [Emphasis on family]

Frank Castleton, a successful employee of TVA and later special assistant to Franklin D. Roosevelt, suffers a nervous breakdown and is held "prisoner" in a government hospital because he knows too much. A psychiatrist and a nurse pry from Frank the story of his life, which includes the accumulation of land in Clinch County, Tennessee, family land, which he sold to become rich.

Lentz, Perry. *The Falling Hills* (1967) [Emphasis on place]

Fort Pillow massacre in West Tennessee in 1864. A realistic portrayal of the historic roots of civil rights controversies. The two chief characters are a Tennessee lawyer and Confederate officer and a Union officer from Boston.

Sanguinetti, Elise. *The Last of the Whitfields* (1962) [Place, Family emphases]

Thirteen-year-old Felicia lives in a small Georgia town, where the genteel, proper Southern atmosphere is being upset by integration problems brought on by Northern interference. Humor and light-hearted irony characterize the first-person account of growing up faced with misunderstanding parents.

———————. *The Dowager* (1968) [Emphasis on place]

The "dowager" is the city of Charleston, whose personality is delineated in the pages of the novel. Winky Carr, age 25, cannot believe that it was merely a summer romance, but as she settles into the familiar routine in Charleston and waits for a letter from Walter, time passes without a word from him. She retreats further behind the walls of security in the city.

———————. *The New Girl* (1964) [Emphasis on place]

Felicia Whitfield, of *The Last of the Whitfields,* goes to an exclusive boarding school in Virginia. The story of Felicia, age 15, is almost a girl's version of *The Catcher in the Rye.* In addition to the account of events in Felicia's life, a cheating scandal, a death, and a tragedy, the novel reflects changing racial attitudes in the South.

Smith, Lee. *The Last Day the Dogbushes Bloomed* (1968) [Place, Family emphases]

Nine-year-old Susan Tobey loses her innocence and has her first experience of evil. The setting is the South in the 1930s. Susan's father is devoted to her, but her mother deserts her family and runs off with another man. Susan's sister becomes engaged, and Susan is terrorized by a vicious and cruel little boy.

———————. *Fancy Strut* (1973) [Emphasis on place]

The citizens of the town of Speed, Alabama, in the 1960s, are planning a sesquicentennial celebration. They want to become a part of the "New" South. It is a stereotyped picture of a Southern town and of Southerners, with alcoholism, adultery, attempted suicide, bigotry, drugs, insanity, promiscuity, and riots.

Stallworth, Anne Nall. *This Time Next Year* (1972) [Emphasis on family]

Florrie Birdsong's mother yearns for the city, and Florrie, age 15, is torn between her love for her father, the farm, the woods, and her admiration for her mother. Toliver, her father, is a tenant farmer in Alabama during the Depression.

____________. *Where the Bright Lights Shine* (1977) [Emphasis on family]

In contrast to the dream of Florrie Birdsong's mother, Callie Berryhill achieves her dream of leaving the farm and buying a house in Birmingham. But her husband Snow is a dirt farmer and is irresistibly drawn back to the cotton field he loves. Callie's single-minded struggle to pay the monthly mortgage for her dream drives both Snow and their three daughters from her.

FICTION IN THE AGRARIAN TRADITION: FOUR THEMES

*Indicates works discussed in this introduction

1. A Sense of Place

Bell, Robert E., *The Butterfly Tree*
*Brown, Joe David, *Stars in My Crown*
Campbell, William March, *A William March Omnibus*
__________, *Come in at the Door*
__________, *The Tallons*
__________, *The Looking-glass*
__________, *The Bad Seed*
Coleman, William Laurence, *Adam's Way*
__________, *Escape the Thunder*
Covin, Kelly, *Hear That Train Blow*
Deal, Babs H., *Acres of Afternoon*
__________, *It's Always Three O'Clock*
__________, *Night Story*
__________, *High Lonesome World*
__________, *The Walls Came Tumbling Down*
__________, *The Grail*
Deal, Borden, *The Winner*
__________, *The Insolent Breed*
__________, *The Advocate*
__________, *Interstate*
__________, *The Tobacco Men*
*Kelley, Welbourn, *Alabama Empire*
*Murray, Albert, *Train Whistle Guitar*
*Sanguinetti, Elise, *The Dowager*
__________, *The Last of the Whitfields*
Smith, Lee, *Fancy Strut*
__________, *The Last Day the Dogbushes Bloomed*
*Stewart, John Craig, *Through the First Gate*
*Warren, Lella, *Whetstone Walls*

2. The Importance of the Family

*Brown, Joe David, *Stars in My Crown*
__________, *The Freeholder*

Campbell, William March, *Come in at the Door*
__________, *The Tallons*
Coleman, William Laurence, *Orphan Jim*
__________, *Clara*
__________, *King*
__________, *Beulah Land*
Deal, Bab H., *High Lonesome World*
*Deal, Borden, *The Other Room*
__________, *The Advocate*
__________, *The Least One*
__________, *The Insolent Breed*
__________, *Dunbar's Cove*
Huie, William Bradford, *In the Hours of Night*
*Murray, Albert, *Train Whistle Guitar*
*Sanguinetti, Elise, *McBee's Station*
__________, *The Last of the Whitfields*
Smith Lee, *The Last Day the Dogbushes Bloomed*
Stallworth, Anne Nall, *This Time Next Year*
__________, *Where the Bright Lights Shine*
Stewart, John Craig, *Through the First Gate*
Warren, Lella, *Whetstone Walls*

3. Moral and Religious

*Brown, Joe David, *Stars in My Crown*
*Deal, Borden, *The Other Room* (against organized religion)
*Stewart, John Craig, *Through the First Gate*
*Warren, Lella, *Whetstone Walls* (against organized religion)

4. Man on the Land

Brown, Joe David, *The Freeholder*
*Coleman, William Laurence, *Orphan Jim* (anti-farm)
__________, *Beulah Land*

*Deal, Borden, *The Other Room*
__________, *Dragon's Wine*
__________, *Walk Through the Valley*
__________, *Dunbar's Cove*
__________, *The Least One*

Henderson, George Wylie, *Ollie Miss*
Huie, William Bradford, *In the Hours of Night*
*Sanguinetti, Elise, *McBee's Station*
Stewart, John Craig, *Through the First Gate*
Warren, Lella, *Whetstone Walls*

BIBLIOGRAPHY

Bell, Robert E. *The Butterfly Tree.* Philadelphia: Lippincott, 1959.

Brown, Joe David. *Addie Pray.* New York: Simon & Schuster, 1971.

__________.*The Freeholder.* New York: Morrow, 1949.

__________.*Stars in My Crown.* New York: Morrow, 1947.

Campbell, William Edward March. *The Bad Seed.* New York: Rinehart, 1954. (New York: Dell, 1972).

__________. *Come in at the Door.* New York: H. Smith & R. Haas, 1934.

__________.*The Looking-glass.* Boston: Little Brown, 1943.

__________.*The Tallons.* New York: Random House, 1936.

__________. *A William March Omnibus.* New York: Rinehart, 1956.

Capote, Truman. *The Grass Harp, and A Tree of Night and Other Short Stories.* New York: New American Library, 1956.

Coleman, Lonnie (William Laurence Coleman). *Adam's Way.* New York: Dutton, 1953.

__________. *Beulah Land.* New York: Doubleday, 1973.

__________. *Clara.* New York: Dutton, 1952.

__________. *Escape the Thunder.* New York: Dutton, 1944.

__________. *King.* New York: McGraw-Hill, 1967.

__________. *Orphan Jim.* New York: Doubleday, 1975.

Covin, Kelly. *Hear That Train Blow.* New York, Delacorte, 1970.

Deal, Babs H. *Acres of Afternoon.* New York: D. McKay, 1959.

__________. *The Grail.* New York: D. McKay, 1963.

__________. *High Lonesome World: The Death and Life of a Country Music Singer.* Garden City: Doubleday, 1969.

__________. *It's Always Three O'Clock.* New York: D. McKay, 1961.

__________. *Night Story.* New York: D. McKay, 1962.

__________. *The Reason for Roses.* New York: Doubleday, 1974.

__________. *The Walls Came Tumbling Down.* Garden City: Doubleday, 1968.

Deal, Borden. *The Advocate.* Garden City: Doubleday, 1968.

———. *Dragon's Wine.* New York: Scribner, 1960.

———. *Dunbar's Cove.* New York: Scribner, 1957.

———. *The Insolent Breed.* New York: Scribner, 1959.

———. *Interstate.* Garden City: Doubleday, 1970.

———. *The Least One.* New York: Doubleday, 1967.

———. *The Loser.* New York: Doubleday, 1964.

———. *The Other Room.* New York: Doubleday, 1974.

———. *The Spangled Road.* New York: Scribner, 1962.

———. *The Tobacco Men.* New York: Holt, Rinehart & Winston, 1965.

———. *Walk Through the Valley.* New York: Scribner, 1956.

———. *The Winner.* New York: Doubleday, 1973.

Henderson, George Wylie. *Ollie Miss.* New York: Frederick A. Stokes Co., 1935. (Chatham, N.J.: Chatham Bookseller, 1973.)

Huie, William Bradford. *In the Hours of Night.* New York: Delacorte, 1975.

Kelley, Welbourn. *Alabama Empire.* New York: Rinehart, 1957.

Lentz, Perry. *The Falling Hills.* New York: Scribner, 1967.

Murray, Albert. *Train Whistle Guitar.* New York: McGraw-Hill, 1974.

Sanguinetti, Elise. *The Dowager.* New York: Scribner, 1968.

———. *The Last of the Whitfields.* New York: McGraw-Hill, 1962.

———. *McBee's Station.* New York: Holt, Rinehart & Winston, 1971.

———. *The New Girl.* New York: McGraw-Hill, 1964.

Smith, Lee. *Fancy Strut.* New York: Harper & Row, 1973.

———. *The Last Day the Dogbushes Bloomed.* New York: Harper & Row, 1968.

Stallworth, Anne Nall. *This Time Next Year.* New York: Vanguard, 1972.

———. *Where the Bright Lights Shine.* New York: Vanguard, 1977.

Stewart, John Craig. *Through the First Gate.* New York: Dodd